The 'Ophelia' Prophecies

Dustin Pickering

Love's Philosopher

for *sufferers of Borderline Personality Disorder.*
"Your memory remaineth stilled, although without order and cause: the higher castes revolve the veils of spiritual war."

Table of Contents

Editor's note: Mr. Pickering has chosen to not give titles to several pieces contained in this manuscript, we honor his intention.

Dustin Pickering

"And will he not come again?...No, no, he is dead;

Go to thy deathbed."

- Act IV, Scene V, 'Hamlet'.

Introduction

This intense collection of poetry is the spawn of what appears to be a world in peril, a world in tears, a broken world and a confused world. The contemporary spiritual crises adorning our doors and gates of the heart infect all the human condition. Pandemic, threat of war, global unrest and economic depressions, personal turmoil within relationships, and narcissism and glib personalities running the world and taking advantage of the named crises are contributing to human despair at record rates.

It is concerning and alarming that personal relationships are suffering as well as the national lives. There is no comfort in much but distraction. As the Bible says, the more you know the more you increase your suffering. We are all Hamlet.

For those wise fools who don't have the ultimate answers but recognize the imminent collapse and regard it as a deeply hidden excess of evils behind the veil, this collection will provide beauty and faith. The great renaissance is at hand.

-Dustin Pickering, 2022

a mind of utter epoch

why is g.d's name love and why did you
take the bitter fowl from my eyes,
plucking the string
and emptying the threshold
from ruination? Epoch so stain'd by shadow
in the restless contempt.

The holy spirit at holy rest.

Catastrophe theory sets the tails aright,
Mountainous epiphany
Stretch of the ace

As the avalanche of forgotten fevers
Utter helpless in down the presence

Why did you empty g.d and call him love?
Why does the teleology not trust my intention?

Rock tumbling the street of sleep.
All things search for their creator,

But why did g.d remove his eyes
From the sight
Of the damned
Why did he not see the humiliation
Rinsed from cold kaleidoscopic eye?

The rainbow extends through the eastern star
From the blessing of deuces
But dictators strive o strive to know the flesh
It's hurting healing horror

Why did you tear g.d from the Cross
And tell him to seek chaos

Dustin Pickering

In sleeping, repose of such unknown...
The quest we dug from out the whispers
        Of old dog faced gods.

The 'Ophelia' Prophecies

for Yemen

if hearing servants in the winter wind
healed the premise from its dividends—
your slavery is something to remedy on its own.

we cannot capitalize on misery
we cannot die on the lightning
we cannot suffer the children in the cauldron
leave all to be heard from the silence

they stifle your voice
with saturated books of irony
and I know you aren't the one to tell me
love is your secret

dark enigma of love,
caulk my heart unto sickness:
this death is annihilation of serene.
is it faith to open wounds
to glue them closed with your eyes?
stitch softness, gloat the emptiness.
i won't hurt your suffering
during love's suicidal drama—
torches of doves dominating the photo.
drop the olive branch down the soul
for command of flaw,
but listen to the wind only as the one.

balance the whore's Assumption
in the hairs of Christ:
know the loincloth as lineage
to the unbecoming.

again we rise, again the day is still.
we don't see the morning star
until her memory freshens,
pollen from particulars enlarging scores.

my mouth is filled with *blasphemes*—
and these terrors don't tress the tree
by the oblivion of your story.

waltz of the damned

diamonds worn on the skin,
diamonds worn in the morning star's brightness:
we are love to loved ones
and together we bark the soul's demolition.

this is together the end of nemesis
where sunflowers reach in torpor
for the Sunday Times.
we are turning to crime on streets of passion--
we are breaking bread with the foreigners.

the crystal ball shadowed black with an angel's wing.

The Animal's Wounds

I'm searching the hours
for signs of love:
I'm searching the rackets
for world and wise.
the privacy of this space
in the hearty father's contemplation,
contemporary though slight—

Fate's eye casts a beam
and all the cold streams turn warm
and my skin blackens with anxiety.
de profundis, the animal's wounds:
gouge out my eyes so I never see
this frost again!

the garden of rue

ivy grows here in solitude.
crowds face the room
where your light was born:
i am fully myself
when beached alone with your heart
on my shoulder.
don't dance again with this rose in teeth.
the death of singing, the mind of faith,
struggle to hear me, struggle to hear me bleed,
don't think when you rip this trance.
just let's dance, let's dance.

Fate is the only woman who wants me,
so it is Fate's rainbow I will chase
to find the destitution of the world
coming alive, again, yes again,

in the yes of the eyes
where the no is forsaken,
your mind is my courage,
my thoughts your insolence:

the fabric is bent, dream, the fabric
is final—blood, the last recourse, war:
you are a woman, o wisdom,
sing!

PART TWO

"Whatever is confined within the limits of a natural
life cannot by its own efforts go beyond its immediate
existence; but it is driven beyond it by something else,
and this uprooting entails its death."
-Hegel's *Phenomenology of Spirit*

St. Paul cast his demons to the largesse—
central trust to the Tao,
he fled to the heavens alone:
and he gave back what came for him.
Fate casts Her dark hook in the angeleyes
letting glances take what they may—
o desperation do you know which way to look?

The 'Ophelia' Prophecies

o mighty angst you have returned
to combat holiness in its stead—
your combustion into rock, O Lucifer,
these little lights so positive to the storm

as you crash the light into starry mist,
union of present to the curtain castcall,
it's the end of the era,
the wall has descended over life's face
like a fog over cold friction.

i stared too much into the light
and now this little dance has prayed
its way to the Patmos of our love.

rip the children from the womb,
again Lord you have tried:
Neptune collapsed her largesse
as shrouded tortures are convey'd:

the angst, the star is riddled,
I am reading your magic, o God of Time,
your flight from reality
is my own death and dying,
I have folded into the waters
and seen the sky as if its blood was high.

the dark room

the dark room is barred
by knotted arms
imagined relationships
friends with benefits
tightened grips

and I thought to enter
like passing through a grotesque painting
from the Baroque era
thin as paper
their arms are polysyllabic phonemes

i cannot break the autonomy of their sins

we speak our own love language
and the translators are x and y

your mind is an enigma
your sexuality is devastating

as a man i am well fed
with lies and paradox

The 'Ophelia' Prophecies

St. Michael

Death strikes me, strident and unaware,
Glorious imp riddled with oceanic feeling,

Her eyes, the ancient sadness convey'd,
Promises of understanding,

Battalions offer this gloom of battle
As I stand beside you anticipating such furor.

And understanding is such a paradox!
You can see the eyes and their depth,

But you cannot hear my mind ticking
Each box, anxious and alarmed,

Virginal shroud of this night where the sea
Bites at the moon's ankles, terror and awe.

St. Michael drags the empty winds to their sources.

Dustin Pickering

Rising of Emptiness

Wings of chariots parsed in the fold,
Her distress something of alienation,

Partial penury of pain, untold fathoms.

These depths weep secretly at midnight,
Arming your final pain and promiscuous pleasure...

When you are free to gambit the gaol,
Fires burn the heart into ashes of terror,

Consume, this light, heritage of the womb.

I take the jagged cliff where it bites
And launch to another sun,

Farewell, this has become too much.

Unknown Arch

Arms are lashed in the gambit.
There are too many creatures
Hiding their sagacity in the bow,

Crux of completeness,
The oasis where your dreaming is abandoned.

Mute me in the shadows,
And torch the silence for oppression's wage,

Handle the night with wounds.

Carousel

Fugitive roses fly across the stolen embankment.
Petal-train in the rising splendor,
So much launched in the seeds:

Your tarot card thinks its own life—
Staved man, your whiteness against the cold pasture,

All swollen thoughts embody the terror of my angel.

Hollowed Ground

If the bleak Rainer would part my lips,
Thought in focus offbeat,
A remedial chaos to usurp pleased eyes,

Our unity in breath, this passing passel
Parted by remnants of cold flight,

Torn between the thought and the deed:
A conscientious steed.

it's the timing of the sickle

we cast out the enemy
from the range of gods
her eyes were empty as patterns
of prayer demolition

steadfast grief autocrats want the system
only for themselves
but you must feel too, o Savior
they must whip and flail you like a slave...

spin the cacophony of the damned
this insolent little thing
your love opened the floods from my eyes
and I was awakening from the touch

The 'Ophelia' Prophecies

i disavowed my nemesis
on television bright and early
the gravity of my eucalyptus
posturing as healing the remnant

it's an environment of transgression
and you abducted my heart from the rain
the subtle Greek leaned against his prayer
in the Stoic wilderness of midnight

and are you fond?
i say, are you fond?

why i stare in disbelief

the acorn was born to a tree
fallen from the oak
and you were born from me, my rib,
like Lucifer the star...

and i slept and wept in anxieties
i did not understand.

when you tell me things i do not believe,
your stream flows through all things—
including the ape of my heart,
the circumstance of my being.

you stood in the garden, questioning.

The 'Ophelia' Prophecies

i was still

in the stall of your heart, dear One,
the fabricated essence of Your will,
cabbaged by the memories branded in far fear.

this is where you had me.

i was still, in the shadows of your palace,
parlanced to the figmentary illusion—
but you, scavenger of surreal, you were One
then Several, then One again, Legions appareled
by strain and force,
yet no one knows the answer to the riddle.

Sphinx-shot by slander and bypassed surrender:
the mind jogs like Job in the whirlwind of rage.

guarded by Pandora's Box

your eyes are lights of opium-wire
staged by splendid vacuums of touch

and the enemy is guarding the gate
where your emerald palace is golden

we kiss. the stage is set for thoughts anew
risked by cultural abandon,

and Hope is Envy's dear cousin for the select,
a general prospect, agitations and flames.

her Evolution is spectacular game, foraged for error,
slight provocations still the shadows.

PART THREE

did you hear God's eye
scream the tunnel of night
across moons of miracles?

if the sea remembers—
let it fit into the cauldron—
and let it eagerly take its fills
from the circuitous route.

the sweetheart's diction

we wait for war in the parallel,
clouded visions and fears,
thoughts of the winter open the shields.

buxom beauty of war, deceiver of many woes,
harbinger of gross deceit and net profits,
liberty dethroned from the town square!
do we need a remedy of the source?

G.d waits in the aperture, light digging the silence
into its vapid increases of foolishness—
hell is brought upon us, a declaration,
thematic glory invites your prestige.

i can only follow the diction, the rules
promulgated by syntax and cleverness—
war in the parallel cycling to the end,
address your faith.

follower of followers

does love politicize our ways,
the social moniker where eyes
eat the vagina,
that tiny corpuscle of the anus—

o wickedness, do not fear your demise!
The trumpets fallow the soul
where epitome waits, guarded by cherubs
rocking the boat.

cherubs do not know the bell,
for the tolling bell sympathizes
with a great humanity.
and since death is on the front covers,
endtimes approaching,
the Fall is also the Resurrection.

Eyes Remain Dry

It hurts me to make a good woman cry,
her eyes swell like fonts at the river of blessing.

It hurts me to see a man in pain,
in tears, counting his blessings.

And it hurts me to know we all cause this pain,
without intending,

and we so often, more often than not, ignore it
when we do: yet we want sympathy when we cry.

How are eyes to remain dry in the valley of tears?

The Anti-Climax (Hope Springs Eternal)

Natural rhythm of life,
defying the spectrum of co-existence:
formal apologies not accepted
due to personal judgment.

We were in sync, lips parted ways
after parroting symphonies of grudge.
An enemy is fuel to the tongue.
Fight the mad blistering of time.

You were of my essence:
we must leave the church of being
for the crater of the anticlimatic—
your senses are stunned with glory

and the fruit is rotting on the bough.

Dustin Pickering

Sleep and Waking

You are priceless like a handful of stars;
the treasure of time is bountiful for your love.

You hold me in your mind like a windswept dream.
The reality of love is deep, deeper than snow.

Our kiss in the tunnel of light left us singing.
Perpetually we shift roles in the basking.

Your kindness to me is candy and family
to my longing and grim delight.

I am mischievous like the ocean of sound
before the fall of a wave.

You cuddle me into sleep and wait
for my waking mind to tell you kind things—

in the sheep's bath we strain our ears
to gather one another from the bed.

Hearken to the Flood

Her wasted eyes careful and serene,
the tales they protect,
the lives they guard.

She is older than the ancients.
Their tears flood the dark
with solemn gesticulation.

Her minstrelsy guides them
to the rain of faces.
Everyone is new here—
there are no blood lovers
in this lake of fire.

You do not sing louder
than the apple of my eyes—
that touch of forgiveness,
the right to suffer abuse

and not tell the tale.

Gift of Parting

What does Death look like in my arms of plastic?
Does He grovel in the charm of insolence?

Is God awake at this ungodly hour?
Attending my wishes and keeping the silence intact?

When the crystal gazes back,
do you know the river?
An old crispness to the apple,
and tongue of parting.
Such is the life of dream
and the death of circumstance.

Your Eyes

Your irises reach out like a baby's fist,
clenching the wise old world as a new fool.

We all strive for some sanctimonious garb,
something to alight our dim brow with meaning.

Your eyes, no artifice, are forbidden words spoken
near the crying child of fear and forgetting.

Our children are holding flowers in the dusky auroras
of time, where your eyes love the graces of my flowing body.

When you look at me with starving lusts and thoughts,
I remember your eyes are clenching fists seeking a golden
room.

Science of Being

The night in fractal purity
spins and enchants.
We are together at last, after lazy September
captures the mosquitoes of our dreams.

Your magical sundry offers a glimpse into sight.
A miscellany of mirth and mangrove.
You live in the moments of silence.

In a net of fear of abandonment,
I wait to silence the luxury of your arms:
into the quietest of senses your mind quakes,
designing vengeance and abhorring bigotry.

What is closest to you in heart,
that is the thing that makes the body revolt.

Out of the Twisted Tree
for Yeats

Out of the twisted tree
comes unity and harmonious freedom.
The gyres turn in togetherness.

Things dissolve and the center does not hold—
absolute unity is the curator of madness's dream.

Nature breaks the wings at Babel,
the Tower falls and shrinks the humanity.

Out of the twisted tree
the past sings harmoniously—
again, and again, and again.

The renaissance renews and makes anew.

Trees are historians of nature
and they keep watch over their own.
They know the carbon footprints of thousands of years.

The years walk and they are silent.
In a need for community we create language,
leaving our stamp on the world
as we whisk away to heaven.

When the Tower falls, it is the tree
that gathers it by the roots.
Languages deep in sorrow at inevitable failure—
the mission to bridge the world
becomes the roots at which we balance
our blanching fears.

Beyond the twisted tree—

there is singing, death, toads of the malady.
In the forest, we return to our deep well-being.

The tower collapses on us, languages devour
our risks and bend to the roots that bore them.
Unity is an impossible dream.

A Game of Marbles

Tacit he flicks
game like crucifix—
not a yawn,
not a cheat,
but recourse to the source

where pain travels like doubt.

In his hotel room
his strategic ignorance
offers Dagny's frustration
the collateral required.
Bright boy, brilliant mind,
closes the deal
                feigning slack judgment.

He does nothing out of place.
What is burning the city—
virtue or reward?

Lustful Reproach

her spurious senseless eyes:
dog of the fruit

where boughs peak across black.
eternally adolescent,

in the drifter's lamp
where being slight slumps

into the bright rumps
of the wanderer.

simple cotton of your breath:
the stars flight focus the breening arch,

branched to the perfection of hogback.
composed complacent,

in the rant of ramp
where unknowing fight thumps

the final bliss of plump
bosom, the bright particle.

raindrop

homage to Afghanistan

spider-eye this luminescent hole.
if thoughts are only rigmarole.
fall strike the timpani where tampon-light
floods the beast of meat, this whistling whinny.

drink the flesh where her eyes roll tom,
the beam of worship from church of bomb,
'ere the only catch is distance,

airdrifter the *Magician* knows—
His speech juxtaposes poise and actual,

a faith only welcomed by presidential pardon.

The world an egg withdrawing
as yolk falls from shells

like pushed assault rifles in the piffle of promise.

This rape of the polity will not be forgiven.
Afghan eyes, we miss the hope devout.

Your spirit'd slumber knows not the broken.

Me and Job

> "Do you give the horse his might?"
> Job 39:19

Me and Job, we gettin' along!
The world is in a slump
but I got the best friend of anyone.

He got fried, he's like my cousin
who died in war....
That serious shit ain't the flattering thing.

Extraordinary claims offer their best evidence
in this trial of existence.
O, if anything goes it will.

I won't attend Job's funeral
if he can't attend mine.
I tell the world we ain't alive—

the asskissers of politics
and meanspirits of time
cannot keep me and Job away.

No Pearls to Peal

There is no pearl in purgatory
No pearls for the dream of me
No pearl I can find that was mine eye
I will hide in the dustbowl of Eden
Sweet summary of distance the keepers sleep
I do not see though cold blindness alights me
Battering the bliss of its own fountain

High sun of tomorrow in the cartoon flesh
Ineffable dreamer in mental havoc of laughter
A day's drive through the mountain of sorrow
Tender is this loss where grief is rescinded...
No one will love us so we won't know
Paradise is not something we know
Not a friend in world, not a damn one

We look for the lost but hell is nowhere a dream
Do you even torture time's rainbow?
View this bliss from afar 'cos it ain't coming back

Inflation

Modern monetary supply baffles
like a balloon intent on decrying space
but who huffs this drug anymore?
Faith in currency is love of money.

If I had to refute the illimitable dollar
I would crucify it to its own strategy.
Money, your unsound arrogance murders
the listless humanity of mind.

The more value you impart by number
the less value in real terms we remember
as history casts a sideling glare at our gait.
Centralize the sought in all that is bought.

How do we redeem ourselves in this land
where paper coupons are robust,
and financial literacy is a bust
on a boom cycle? Congress shrugs.

Don't look to me for guidance.
I teach nothing, only offer a parable.
In poverty you spend more.
When more's to spend, your country is poor.

Erewhon Night

Utopian bliss until the clandestine piece
fades this place of arms,
a bending touch from alms' arc:

when gravity seeks semblance of decease,
the pistons of plight's pinnacle
plan the pleasures of power.

Pressed against as tools of slaughter ceas'd—
desirous of futility but fertile with rose
where Erewhon, blissful nowhere,

does not, and cannot, live to its dusty madness.

Dustin Pickering

The Latecomers

They understood those unfortunate souls
cast from the demon-pit, icily clad in stars.

Relieved from flaming desires,
believers anew offer ripe hesitancy.

When suffering is ignoble the land is barren—
but when a being shoulders the wisdom of children

with the experience of a old man in agony,
that being becomes poet. *Conscious* of eternal place,

chance and destiny meet at one point
on the emblazoned two-dimensional plane.

Freud's Riddle

Love is one's orientation in the world—
to love, one must know wholeness!

Work is one's sublimation of love—
to work, one must be apart!

Work is toward the world
and love is within it.

Politics
to J.B.

Mediocrity is Fate's pat on the back
of a country losing the catalepsy of heart—
the heart, no longer beating, pastes outside its form.
Mediocrity is when you blame doppelgangers
for your own insipid recourse.

Politics is when Mediocrity cuts your feet off
so you can no longer walk.
You instead try to love your enemy as yourself
but your enemy is unearthing your soul
before you. Everything is personal again.

I don't know about you but I prefer water
to this insidious grind of problematics:
strains of song are heard in all ideology
but the song is cast in a dubious play,
palsied by the sweet scent of loss.

Under its weight, imperialism strains decadent:
implying forfeiture in its claims, militarism repeals
the defense of agony's sport.
When *you* are in a losing port— clabber the climb
until ideology is truth, and politics is left behind.

Untitled Misanthropic Ballad

How I despise blemished know-it-alls:
what little they know, they recall
from the pasty mess of reading
not experience of bleeding,
or an understanding of self-deceiving.

How I despise the chic hipster clan:
they follow bent paths in their stand
but such daring-do lacks frank intent.
In a sense, their innocence is tailored to resent;
their readymade sympathy as such is indecent.

How I despise cheap failures addicted to smut
forming calluses in their rotted ruts
where malice hides and claims the dream.
Jealousy is a creature comfort of the redeemed
but what does malice give in return for spleen?

How I despise wealth unearned and poverty that burns
holes in pockets like mine— I, who cannot discern
the learning from what is learned:
a pocket drooping from too much is a miser's chance
to overcome the worries of insignificance.

You wonder why I cannot stay heady
to despise the wealth of the greedy
who take alms from the needy...
forsooth, it is more my mischief
to coax deceit from hidey-holes of grief.

#Hope

Pain is silent shuddering, eyes
closed so thought courses thru hidden
venues of the soul
where all roads meet in devastation.

Her dreams are scattered white light
across worlds of apathy. The mind is imprisoned
in its own decadent joys like a flightless bird.
When the crucible is lifted her thoughts become sincere.

Justice will not bow at hope's promise.
Illusions must be devoid of theatrics;
otherwise, the world would crack its morning lips
like a summer vase with roots outgrowing.

The 'Ophelia' Prophecies

Veni Vidi Vici

A park in vicinity of glory,
trees starved by shadows where grief abounds,
the conqueror once was god.

He refuses to respect his hubris
as midnight strolls along.
Instead he fills a cup with rain
and ink spills from his mouth
like light from a cave.

Dustin Pickering

Purple Pangloss

Inebriated by genteel compunction,
stalwart still life in vagary,
his throat catches the gloom and rips asunder
lyrical passions where rests the Dynamo.

The Mind's Ulterior Door

Empty drawers of consciousness
where linger the scent of cherries.
Her face is only drawing awareness from deep shadow.

If the mind is composed tripartite,
how do doors lift angels from the floor?
Once one leaves this space afresh,
a breeze assaults your genitals.

The man within is quiet. He is the central interlocutor
of *osmeridae* testimony. An iron statue to broken waters.

Flesh of my corpse which knows unheard direction.

Meeting on the Subway

Her eyes are golden and glowering
like a nighttime thief on the hill,
waiting for her fill of the waters
the rivers bring to the sill.

She glances out the window for eternity.
Only the subway shudders below her feet.
Stars make mischief with my hair
caught in her nightgown, written by fleet.

Merciful Fear

Speak to us of whimpering.
Speak to us of the dry melancholy of life
while spring blooms at our feet
and the rain pours across cold lands.

Fear embarks in a journey to discover
only itself, the lyricist of its own haunting.
Yes, fear haunts itself. Haunting oneself
is the coolest liberty of winds to come.

While knowing is what time teaches,
is it worth the ugliness of scars?
Are scars the way we chasten ourselves
in the dawning of an era? No, not at all.

Dustin Pickering

The Cheerful Nazi

My brother wears the star
while you pretend to cry
as if mocking his hideous fear.
Only a child, only a brother to me,
to you he is the fruit of poison.

Don't be afraid of the darkness.
It is only the space between you
and the Creator-- the empty void
where we each face our own shriveled
Holocaust, distance like a wall

in the vastness of crying cosmic space.
His voice is one of blunt rage.
O Father, o vengeance, spare us the fear
of wickedness as we snuff out
like candles in Your reign of blood.

Ordocapitalism

Sometimes intervention, sometimes State:
ordocapitalism is the new blank slate.
Slacken and protract the economics of fate:
with the Commandments broken on the hill, we wait.

Dustin Pickering

Afghanistan today and tomorrow

dark-suited hypnotist in a Pandora box
light of hearts sacrificed to the symposium of time
quenched paradoxes of angel and human
broken resolutions across rivers of guilt
stone of tomorrow in the eye of faith

mother of tempestuous impulse brought to her knees
milk of salvation poured on heads balding with glory
brooding the pretension of sad-square abstinence
i brood on magical thinking's impotence
the slot machine of reality bankrupts again

The 'Ophelia' Prophecies

what is your mother's name?

can i guess by the scent of roses
  on your breath?
the angel-shape you wear on your lapel?

her kisses are the skeletons of rubric
and the anatomy of time
water passes through her eyes

can i guess by how surprised you are?
does knowledge carry a secret handshake?
knives in the kitchen do not tell lies.

amethyst mercies cover her skies.
only she knows your middle name.
life is vanity but at least it is not shame.

anchor of night (a war song)

it is tiring to hear your eyes
speak languages like fruit on the vine.
we want for rations.

we hold the bar of teaching
across winter's highway
while drunken soldiers philander at midnight.

captured in a prison of their own havoc,
the meager moths of time burn softly.
a candle wakens at the last appetites.

let us bake cakes for the quiet ones.
their hands do not appear limpid...
yet mischief is made by barrels of contempt.

final dressing

look deeper into the pit of tears.
her knowledge is deeper than yours
and you sense it.

autodidacts do not resonate their tempers
with lights of another's faith.

*

such light is banquet of the sky.

*

next laughters are logics of fear.
we do not understand imperatives
when bliss is the final dressing.

an effigy of woke

luminescent perplexing time sweetness
natural saccharine of life's dunes
amassing the behavioral characteristics
    of brownshirts
right and left
left and right
                but whatever it is
                it is not awake

imperial dogma

      power comes from the circle
void of instantaneous wreckage
  this harmony is pyramidal balance

i lay on this bed of stone
left entirely to my own
those who cast have pearls for eyes
and shining stars never blamed
  for the fields of fear.

*

dream of time

Bone Cannibal

He the King ate our bones.
We have no repairs to our homes.
Our water is brown and musty.
Life in the colony is misery.

He the King eats our meats.
He the King is a litany of losses.
He recreates hopelessness every day.
We are mere signs of the way.

The King is language and its finery.
The radical expressions of our hearts
are invigorated by Romantic ideas.
The calculus will differentiate our blame.

The King will remain the same.

The 'Ophelia' Prophecies

long lilac night

the night smells like purple wishes,
thinkers amidst the lore of food.

sweaty pearls like crusted eyes,
we witness her thoughts as vanity.

cold animals are conundrums of paper,
origami goons sequestered by wind.

in this long lilac night, our teeth
chatter like windowglass shaking during fear.

if envy writes your courage
across the sky of a listening ear:
remember, remember where you visit in flight.
talk to pleasant beings with humanity of sight.

service reaches across the demanding dawn
where people shrug their shoulders in uncertain faith.
dementia is the player's laugh at long last.
talk to pleasant beings with humanity of past.

if envy insists on tearing you to bits,
remember its teeth are old and brittle.
it will find another resource soon to imperil.
talk to pleasant beings with humanity of will.

i am friends with the world
where work is play and dream is sleep
where i am left in broken pieces to reconstruct
where i am supposed to have eloquent speech

The Falling

the fall season arrives like flame
and the gods are dead.
i wait for devils
in golden regalia of death and misery.
fall is the season of Falling…

my arms are pitched dark from evil's encroachments.
as reject from a world of promises and hopes,
heaven's clouded realm 'unarbitrary and pure,'
i enthrone myself by ecstatic emptiness.
in full regalia, the lettered world calls me sad and imperfect:
in full regalia, women reject me as the worst of men.
my rags are stained satin amusements to the stars.

i am waiting for God to turn me away
so i may satisfy my boring appetites—
i will not worry if i am not invited to the heavenly feast.

rest, angels of oblivion: grief is shelter for the weary.
the gods dictate our fate with candor and cruelty—
such a season is not the one we are prone to forget!

in darkest hours, we remember the primordial ooze
from which strife borne us in cold pontification.
Art breeds into Science from the scene of our wracked
nervousness.

sunlight strikes the mirror and dust settles to bludgeon
illusions
we hold as masses: existence is called the great hoax.
satyrs bleed onto the papers of our most astute yearnings.

who is mankind? what drying eyes deepen the compassion
of rage in this frantic kitsch! frying through this rage,
Nox aeterna smashes the temple of our most sacred stupidities.

the moral arc

longitude and latitude
determine the nature
of how and to what i whisper.

translucent and unkind, this torpor
of life where behemoth meets the squalors
of lordly peace. i often drown in deluge of drafts.
your shoulders, my love, are every justice to me.
i do not make decisions for Fate if an open circuit
requires my input.

the moral arc is long and it covers buildings,
banks, and desperados. shadow, shadow bliss.
they were right to keep the flame alive
but wrong to toss the books inside.

Oblivious to Bullets

They fire at me and seek my strength…
However my diet is skim milk and fruits
That mobilize my main mind against fuckery.
Autonomy is my creatine and folly
While I sing the song of imprisoned children.

I respond to the agenda and I look into the void.
Nothing in this life is consistent except the slave-keys.
Music is my medicine and I think in terms of fear.
These days I am gone!

The yonder yokels of time's turning
Want changes in the grid.
They do not understand the mathematics of distance.
Ratios compile and complain.
Humantimes this trend of terror!

I am going into different circles
To approach this question.
I must add one favor. Leave me alone.

On Irrational Testimony: Celine's Engagement with
Darkness
for Neil Silberblatt

What contradiction is born here?
Am I individual, collective? Atom or entity?
Do not worry, friend, for the truth will reckon in the end.
The collective will allow space for Being
and room for Becoming. You will reach toward the ether
in fathomless stretches. Your arms will be guided by the hand
which is guided by fingers. Learn to balance your joy.

In death, darkness will cede to light:
your journey to the end will bear the truth it refused
yet refined.
Once you are witness to this light, carry on, and do not
wound
with the eyes the tasteless vision of eternity.
Truth is elemental and rules with its soft hands and habits.
The celestial ribbon ties the ugly with the remarkable.
The dialectics of change are forever engaged in remorseless
battle.

Walk your street in solitude and random contemplations.
Such randomness is the stuff of the world, the wreck of faith
that brings vision and scratches veneer from the dark.
Scrape the blindness of appearances and shift the world.
Uncover what is to be.

I have not seen the argument yet I know it exists.
Perchance I am to reckon with the Absurd?
Is the Absurd unseen particulate matter
that constitutes our resistance?

The 'Ophelia' Prophecies

Acting as security patrol,
distance invites the familiar into
one's agonish fields:
moral stances accumulate like trash
on crimson highways.
Suicide reveals most of the memories
from the kitsch casino.
I bring a stone like a brother.
Weight is bomb of wearisomeness.

Like a snitch in armor,
her body told me things I did not want told.
She moved in the ways our ancestors moved—
something unseen reminded me of her seductive securities.

Calm and casual, she paced the musical measures
of thought and season.
Her voice was like a piano stroked gently by maestros
superior in the art of love.

Underneath the measured glance
and the theater of cruelty,
she is the Sun to planetary life.
Her eyes are apples plucked for sin.

Her legs sent raptures of apostasy
down my martyred brow:
She dressed in gowns and sleep,
adorned as Papacy's laden.

Swift riff of circumspection—
in tandem her hero waits with aching breath.
Together they were hung by the State
as love's mere idolatry.

The 'Ophelia' Prophecies

For Ukraine

And what if the flames consume you,
what then of the fallacy?
How do the visions retire?

Like an unborn river in the temple,
minds seeking anonymity—
and what crime is felt by the dodge?

Sweet opium distilled, the dame of fuckery,
this thickened castration by the unheard.
Sit *sans* revolution, *sans* atomic, *sans* nuclear—

and realize your crime of passion,
if trust wept the eyes on your dresses,
lonesome fears, the sword of Damocles descending.

Let go of the rattling—such
is mythology, the rape and undying,
a human feat beyond wounds.

Once the gaze strangely flays the ambivalence
where the fractured partisans offer baptismal rites
a fractal fathom of suicide sits strangled—such innocence.

Anarchy's threads tie the empty innate to desecrate—
such pathos of child's cries, sympathy for the good blue.
If this will not oppose such sanctimony lamb where matrices
flash,
the ancient laws of gravity will usurp blinding heat:
and theft of callous torch, tiki of death—
and nihilism of purpose. But what does this sing, sing, of it?

What you know, devil, to exploit our ruthless axe,
for blood it held, kept safe the stove of meat.
We are nothing but strangers to this ancient work

that excuses with recues the nothing of an embryo.
Wait for the kill to tell its joke, you want the bounty—
and yes, my renaissance will rip the world from its famous
work
and I have cast the devil to the sky, becoming free.

Did the Cyclops think my stare was perpetual?
And you aren't balanced on the tip
because such catalyst is fraud.
Do you think ideality has ignored you?
Yet the tremor in my hand gaslights my own proxy war.

A slouch due to moral weakness,
his eye the cuneiform of monsters,
his back bulges as he records shadows
with the utensil of mind.
When he eats the dark puppets
as everything vanishes, ghosts achieve
feathery holidays in solemn waters.
Conscious of his lusts and memories
the luminary prankster plies orgasm
with fish and failed swimmers.

And his body is a ship of fools
porting at a moment of hesitancy
while other men's wives are settling
for pans of fool's gold.

I will hang myself in the bedroom of your heart
like a photograph yellowing behind a thin frame.
And you will sleep with my eager expression
in pausation, telling you stories of my woes.
And my abandoned hopes fly from their cages.

My eyes blue as sapphires, translucent in tears.
Such that coral is their undergarment.
When I am in my stoic nakedness the dark will
clothe my body, leaving silence as a distant rune.

In the morning of my yellow hair,
stars retract their promises
and oaths are gray with breaking wishes;
the broken silence is my last sleep.

The 'Ophelia' Prophecies

I am concerned with the month of January,
it's seemingly ubiquitous Tantalus configured
by restriction and ballyhoo.
These nights lifted by day's end through the moniker
of fear and fantasy—
as illusion passes from its shuttlecock
into divisions by diurnal sympathy.
The path of retribution is false and forgotten.
This last moment is held by staring eyes.

As the juxtaposition of stint with rapt joy
shouldering pain declares unification,
shifting collisions mirror our neurons.
The web of activity does not re-imagine itself
by competence of action.
This semblance of withdrawal from light
aims to forget all slight.

It was the summer of the unloved,
and Sundays of neglect and timeless tortures.
Her bounty this America will dive into your flesh
and recover the mythos of walking depth.
Your flesh is perceived as celebrity
and your status measured carefully
like water dispensed in cups with holes in the bottom.

When I stumble through the glistening path
of narcissistic charm, fearing only the glove of innocence
that wishes to violate my own theater
I sing stillness to the virtual audience of my thoughts.
Because they refuse to care I am mere abortion to the light.

It was the summer of unloving, emptiness, backless burning:
you lit the torch of my honesty in this cosmopolitan dread.
Uncertainty cockstrewn across my heart, blackened to
blisters,
as this universe expands in weight and tutelage.
And when I burn like the straw of my mother's temperament,
illusions disperse throughout the wicked market.
O! But be kind and trust this projected façade.
Gleam from it the shadowed night.

Classrooms offer the purity of silence—
and when you raise your hand to the grind
the imbeciles of dawn smack your plenty
to the oblivion where hearts are thick.
And memory of melodrama is nothing slight.

It was the summer of wishing to be heard.
It was the summer of one thousand blessings
that all meant nothing.
In the dying of this age, my tomb is filled with flowers
of what they wanted from me.

The 'Ophelia' Prophecies

I am not your star anymore, bright locus
of Icarian stripe:
pandemonium eagerness of farce.
And yet the history is a repeat as if recorded by an alcoholic
sleeping in route to the ends of the flat earth.

And this snippet of envy in the diatribe of futility?
Listen to the rocking horse where you held the hand
of torpor, then waking, this is one of the last decades
of anything Either/Or.

With every tryst of light—
the bruises craft illusion
and your breath is the last alter.
If I am to wreck this idol fearful of tears,
I must take the last beating with music in my ears.

The Man Who Sold the World

O God, God,
How weary, stale, flat and unprofitable
Seem to me all the uses of this world!
Hamlet (I.ii.)

Invisible realities are hard to find.
The natural impetus is aloneness
in a cold, dark and bare room
covered in spider webs, roach carcasses,
and signifiers spoken aloud.
Yes, it is He who heard me.
In silence He devastates me.

This stone is one of laughter
like a child scared of a curved blade.
I probe this destitute reality with my voice
but my voice, it echoes back with insincerity.
The ambivalent abortion of mind
snitched to the womb,
still stitched to God in almighty darkness—
this child is me, a Man, hopeless in relentless questions.
You come to me only as a whirlwind
knowing I would slit your uncanny throat myself,
God of unequal torments. Did you die savagely
or was it your son? We speak as equals. Tell me.
Are the flowers from your throat eternal offerings?

You sold me the world and will not take it back.
Love in such pitiless tombs is a blessing secured
to me and my posterity. Take it back, dumb fag,
I did not know it was refuse.

I am left knowing your other dear creatures
fill the same breadlines as me.
We will talk and you will eavesdrop.

Curious spectator you are.
You are right that I did not create the beast
that swallowed me, swallowed all, that State
so preached by Hobbes.
I will speak bluntly for my fellow men, women and children
and all we feel. We are afraid.
Yet you ask to be loved in fear and trembling.
So I offer my own flowers instead of cutting your throat.

About the author

Dustin Pickering is the founder of *Transcendent Zero Press* and founding editor of *Harbinger Asylum,*. He is the author of several poetry collections, a novella, a fairy tale, many short stories, essays, critical reviews, and articles. He was placed as a finalist in *Adelaide Literary Journal's* short story contest in 2017 and honored by *The Friends of Guido Gozzano* in 2020. He is a former contributor to Huffington Post and is the Anchor at Literary Corner at *New York Parrot.* He lives in Houston, Texas.

Acknowledgements

Cover art courtesy of Sarah Hussein

The 'Ophelia' Prophecies

www.ingramcontent.com/pod-product-compliance
Lightning Source LLC
Chambersburg PA
CBHW021955090426
42811CB00001B/39